Preface

The IGNOU MCS-202: Computer Organisation course is an integral part of the Post Graduate Diploma In Computer Applications (PGDCA) curriculum, designed to provide students with a comprehensive understanding of the internal structure, functioning, and principles of computer systems. This course covers critical topics such as computer architecture, data representation, instruction sets, memory systems, and input-output processing, all of which are essential for mastering the workings of a computer system.

This book, IGNOU MCS-202: Computer Organisation Previous Years Unsolved Papers, serves as a valuable resource for students preparing for their examinations. It brings together a collection of unsolved question papers from previous years, allowing students to practice and assess their knowledge on a variety of topics. The unsolved format is aimed at promoting self-assessment and critical thinking, encouraging students to apply the concepts they have learned throughout the course.

By engaging with these unsolved papers, students can explore key areas such as:

Data representation and computer arithmetic
Processor organization and instruction sets
Memory hierarchy, cache, and virtual memory
Input/output systems and interfacing
Assembly language programming
Control unit design and pipelining

Each question paper is structured to mirror the real examination format, giving students an opportunity to familiarize themselves with the types of questions they may encounter. These unsolved papers challenge students to analyze and solve problems, helping them to reinforce their understanding of both theoretical concepts and practical applications.

We hope this book proves to be a beneficial tool for students in their exam preparation and enhances their understanding of computer organization. It is our belief that diligent practice with these papers will enable students to succeed in their academic journey and equip them with the knowledge necessary for future endeavors in the field of computer science.

We would like to express our gratitude to the students and educators who have contributed to the development of this book. Their insights and feedback have been invaluable in ensuring that this compilation meets the highest standards of academic excellence. As you embark on your journey through the world of algorithms, we hope that this book will be a reliable companion in your studies, helping you to unlock the full potential of your capabilities in the field of computer science.

Table of Contents

MCS – 202
Post Graduate Diploma in Computer Applications (PGDCA)
Chapter 1: Term-End Examination, December, 2021
MCS-202 : Computer Organization

Time: 3 Hours
Maximum Marks: 100
Weightage: 70%

Note: Question No. **1** is compulsory and carries 40 marks. Attempt any **three** questions from remaining Questions No. **2** to Question No. **5**.

1. (a) Perform the following operations using signed 2's complement notation of 8 bits (including sign bit). Also indicate overflow, if any : 6
(i) Add – 28 and +127
(ii) Subtract – 56 from – 77
(iii) Add + 28 and + 100

(b) Simplify the following function using K- map : 5
F (A, B, C, D) = $\sum$ (0, 3, 5, 7, 9, 10, 11, 12, 15)
and draw the logic circuit of the function so obtained.

(c) What is the purpose of using cache memory in a computer ? Explain the need of cache mapping scheme. 4

(d) What is the importance of DMA ? Explain its functioning. 5

(e) How is the instruction of a computer different from C language instruction ? Explain various components of a computer instruction. 5

(f) Explain the working of micro-programmed control unit. 5

(g) Explain the components of 8086 micro- processor with the help of a diagram. 5

(h) Write a program using 8086 assembly language that converts a binary value stored in a byte location (assume the value in between 0 and 9) to equivalent ASCII digit. 5

2. (a) Perform the following conversions : 5
(i) $(389)_{10}$ to hexadecimal
(ii) $(FFA)_{16}$ to octal
(iii) $(2357)_{8}$ to hexadecimal
(iv) $(AAA)_{16}$ to decimal

(v) $(235)_8$ to decimal

(b) Draw the block diagram and characteristic table of S-R flip-flop. Make the excitation table from characteristic table of this flip-flop. 5

(c) What is a Master-Slave flip-flop ? Explain its working with the help of a diagram.

(d) Differentiate between Von Neumann and Harvard architecture. 5

3. (a) Why is memory hierarchy created in a computer system ? Explain memory hierarchy with the help of a diagram. 6

(b) Explain the use of interrupt in input/output operation with the help of an example. 6

(c) Why do you need input/output devices ? Explain the functioning of any one output device. 5

(d) Explain the term access time in the context of a hard disk. 3

4. (a) Explain any four addressing modes of a computer with the help of an example of each. 8

(b) What are the advantages of RISC architecture ? Explain the uses of large register file which may be found in RISC with the help of a diagram. 4

(c) Give an example of arithmetic micro- operation and one example of logic micro- operations. 4

5. (a) Explain any **four** instructions of 8086 microprocessor. 8

(b) Explain the following with the help of a diagram/example : 12

(i) Instruction pipeline
(ii) Multiprocessor
(iii) Full adder

MCS – 202

Post Graduate Diploma in Computer Applications (PGDCA-NEW)

Chapter 2: Term-End Examination, June, 2021

MCS-202 : Computer Organization

Time: 3 Hours
Maximum Marks: 100
Weightage: 70%

Note: Question No. **1** is compulsory and carries 40 marks. Attempt any **three** questions from remaining Questions No. **2** to Question No. **5**.

1. (a) Convert the following : 6

    (i) Decimal number 249.125 to binary, octal and hexadecimal

    (ii) Hexadecimal $(FA12)_h$ into octal, binary and decimal

(b) Use K-map to find the optimal function for the function 5

$F(A, B, C, D) = \sum (0, 4, 8, 11, 12, 13)$.

Also draw the logic diagram of resultant function using AND, OR, NOT Gates.

(c) Draw and explain the logic diagram of a RAM cell. 5

(d) A main memory has the size of 2 MB. The word size of the main memory is 16 bits and 1 block of main memory word/cache memory is of 64 bits. The size of the cache memory is 64 KB. Determine the following : 1+1+3=5

(i) Size of the address of main memory.

(ii) The number of cache lines.

(iii) Assuming that a main memory to cache direct address mapping is used, explain how main memory address will be mapped to cache memory address.

(e) Consider the following state of registers and main memory (All values are in Hexadecimal) : 4

Address	Main Memory
4F11	LDA
4F12	4F14
4F13	2567
4F14	6782
4F15	
4F16	4F00
4F17	4F14

Register	Value
AC	2511
IR	
PC	4F11
XR	0002
BR	0003

Assuming that the load instruction is stored in address 4F11 and 4F12, where the location 4F12 contains the address field
of the load instruction. Calculate the value of operand, that would be loaded to AC, if load instruction uses the following
addressing modes :

(i) Memory Direct Addressing
(ii) Index Addressing
(iii) Base Addressing
(iv) Immediate Addressing

(f) Explain the sequence of micro-operations that would be required to fetch an instruction stored in a memory location to
IP register. You may assume that the machine uses MAR → register to stored memory address, R1 → register which stores data received from memory or data to be transferred to memory; AC → register which is used to perform computation, IP → register that stores the instruction, which is fetched and PC → register which stores the instruction to be fetched. Make suitable assumptions. 5

(g) For the following values of various registers in an 8086 microprocessor, compute the physical memory address : 4

(i) CS : IP ≡ 0FABh : 01FAh
(ii) SS : SP ≡ 1F0Ah : 0267h

(h) Write a program in 8086 assembly language that interchanges the value stored in two memory locations having the name FIRST and SECOND. Explain the logic of the program. 6

2. (a) Simplify the following Boolean functions : 4

(i) ((A + B′)′)′ + A . B′
(ii) (A + B)′ + (A . B)′ + (A′. B′)′

(b) Explain the process of error detection and correction using parity bit. 5

(c) Explain the floating point number representation with the help of an example. 5

(d) Explain the working of a basic SR latch. Draw the characteristics table of SR flip-flop. Also make the excitation table of SR flip-flop. 6

3. (a) Explain the internal structure of a hard disk drive with the help of a diagram. 5

(b) Explain the concept of memory hierarchy with the help of an example. 5

(c) What is an Interrupt ? How can it be used for Input/Output ? Explain interrupt driven I/O with the help of an example. 5
(d) Briefly explain any two types of printer technologies. 5

4. (a) Explain the following program control instructions with the help of an example : 2+2+1=5

(i) Branch

(ii) CALL

(iii) Return

(b) What is the need of an interrupt cycle during the instruction execution ? Explain the micro-operations of an interrupt cycle. Make suitable assumptions. 5

(c) Explain the working of Wilkes control unit with the help of a diagram. 5

(d) Explain the use of large register file with the help of an example. 5

5. (a) Explain any three shift instructions in 8086 microprocessor. 6

(b) Differentiate between .com and .exe programs in the context of 8086 microprocessor. 4

(c) Write a program using 8086 assembly language that adds four byte values stored in an array of size 4 in the memory. The result of addition is stored in the fifth and sixth location. 6

(d) Explain the characteristics of the following : 4

(i) Array processing

(ii) Multiprocessor system

MCS – 202

Post Graduate Diploma in Computer Applications (PGDCA-NEW)

Chapter 3: Term-End Examination, December, 2021

MCS-202 : Computer Organization

Time: 3 Hours
Maximum Marks: 100
Weightage: 70%

Note: Question No. **1** is compulsory and carries 40 marks. Attempt any **three** questions from remaining Questions No. **2** to Question No. **5**.

1. (a) Perform the following operations using signed 2's complement notation of 8 bits (including sign bit). Also indicate overflow, if any : 6

(i) Add – 28 and +127
(ii) Subtract – 56 from – 77
(iii) Add + 28 and + 100

(b) Simplify the following function using K- map : 5

$$F(A, B, C, D) = \sum (0, 3, 5, 7, 9, 10, 11, 12, 15)$$

and draw the logic circuit of the function so obtained.

(c) What is the purpose of using cache memory in a computer ? Explain the need of cache mapping scheme. 4

(d) What is the importance of DMA ? Explain its functioning. 5

(e) How is the instruction of a computer different from C language instruction ? Explain various components of a computer instruction. 5

(f) Explain the working of micro-programmed control unit. 5

(g) Explain the components of 8086 micro- processor with the help of a diagram. 5

(h) Write a program using 8086 assembly language that converts a binary value stored in a byte location (assume the value in between 0 and 9) to equivalent ASCII digit. 5

2. (a) Perform the following conversions : 5

(i) $(389)_{10}$ to hexadecimal
(ii) $(FFA)_{16}$ to octal
(iii) $(2357)_{8}$ to hexadecimal
(iv) $(AAA)_{16}$ to decimal
(v) $(235)_{8}$ to decimal

(b) Draw the block diagram and characteristic table of S-R flip-flop. Make the excitation table from characteristic table of this flip-flop. 5

(c) What is a Master-Slave flip-flop ? Explain its working with the help of a diagram. 5

(d) Differentiate between Von Neumann and Harvard architecture. 5

3. (a) Why is memory hierarchy created in a computer system ? Explain memory hierarchy with the help of a diagram. 6

(b) Explain the use of interrupt in input/output operation with the help of an example. 6

(c) Why do you need input/output devices ? Explain the functioning of any one output device. 5

(d) Explain the term access time in the context of a hard disk. 3

4. (a) Explain any four addressing modes of a computer with the help of an example of each. 8

(b) What are the advantages of RISC architecture? Explain the uses of large register file which may be found in RISC with the help of a diagram. 4

(c) Give an example of arithmetic micro- operation and one example of logic micro- operations. 4

5. (a) Explain any four instructions of 8086 microprocessor. 8

(b) Explain the following with the help of a diagram/example : 12

(i) Instruction pipeline
(ii) Multiprocessor
(iii) Full adder

Chapter 4: Mostly Asked Important Questions – Part A

1. Explain Harvard architecture with a diagram, detailing how data and instructions are stored and accessed separately.

Answer: Harvard architecture uses distinct memory and buses for instructions and data, enabling parallel access and reducing bottlenecks compared to the Von Neumann model.

2. Perform number system conversions for:

(i) Decimal to binary, hexadecimal, and octal,

(ii) Hexadecimal to binary, octal, and decimal.

Include sample values and show each step.

Answer: Standard conversion techniques involving division-remainder for decimal to others, and bit grouping or positional values for hexadecimal conversions.

3. Differentiate between CLV and CAV disk organizations, and explain disk access time with the formula and parameters.

Answer: CAV uses constant angular velocity across tracks, leading to consistent data rate; CLV varies rotational speed to maintain density. Disk access time includes seek time + rotational latency + transfer time.

4. Explain memory-mapped I/O, programmed I/O, and Direct Memory Access (DMA). When is DMA preferred over programmed I/O?

Answer: Programmed I/O uses CPU polling; DMA handles data transfers between I/O and memory directly, freeing CPU. DMA is ideal for bulk data transfers.

5. Describe two-way set-associative cache mapping. Provide an example showing how main memory is divided into tag, set index, and block offset.

Answer: Two-way set associative maps each memory block to one of two lines in a set. Address divides into tag, set index, and offset. Blocks can be placed in either line within a set.

6. List register categories in the 8086 microprocessor (e.g., data, address, segment, pointer/index) and explain their roles.

Answer: Categories include general-purpose registers (AX, BX, CX, DX), segment registers (CS, DS, SS, ES), pointer/index (SI, DI, SP, BP), instruction pointer (IP), and flags—each with distinct functions in addressing and control.

7. Compare direct addressing and indirect addressing modes with examples.

Answer: Direct addressing uses the address field in the instruction. Indirect uses the address field to point to a memory location holding the actual address.

8. Explain the structure and logic of an SR flip-flop, including its characteristic and excitation tables.

Answer: SR flip-flop has set (S) and reset (R) inputs. The characteristic table shows next-state based on inputs. Excitation table suggests required input changes to achieve state transitions.

9. Describe addressing modes like register indirect and relative addressing with memory and register examples.

Answer: Register indirect uses a register holding the address of data. Relative uses PC + offset for address computation, common in branch instructions.

10. Write a small 8086 assembly program to interchange two memory values (e.g., FIRST and SECOND). Explain the logic used.

Answer: Typically involves loading one value into a register, swapping, and storing back. Uses instructions like MOV and XCHG for data interchange in memory.

Chapter 5: Mostly Asked Important Questions – Part B

Q1. Explain Harvard architecture with a detailed diagram. Compare it with the Von Neumann architecture, highlighting how separate instruction and data buses improve performance.

Answer: Harvard architecture uses separate memory and buses for instructions and data, enabling simultaneous fetch and execution. This eliminates the Von Neumann bottleneck where a single bus is shared for both instructions and data, causing delays. Harvard's parallel access improves throughput and reduces latency.

Q2. Convert the following: (i) Decimal 873 to binary, (ii) Decimal 384 to hexadecimal, (iii) Hexadecimal FAB to octal, (iv) ASCII string "the escape sequence" to UTF-8 encoding, (v) Octal 765 to decimal. Show each step clearly.

Answer: Decimal to binary is done by dividing the number repeatedly by 2 and recording remainders. Decimal to hexadecimal involves dividing by 16. Hexadecimal to octal requires converting to binary first, then grouping bits into threes. ASCII to UTF-8 uses byte patterns specific to character codes. Octal to decimal applies positional weights.

Q3. Differentiate between CAV and CLV disk organizations. If a disk uses constant angular velocity, explain how access time varies with data location on different tracks.

Answer: CAV spins the disk at a constant speed, leading to higher data rates on outer tracks due to larger circumference. CLV adjusts speed to keep data density uniform across tracks. In CAV, transfer time varies with track position because outer tracks allow more data per rotation.

Q4. Explain two-way set-associative cache mapping with an example. Show how a memory address splits into tag, set index, and block offset.

Answer: In two-way set associative mapping, memory blocks map to one set containing two cache lines. The memory address divides into tag bits, set index bits to locate the set, and block offset bits to locate data within the block. Both lines in the set are checked for tag matches during lookup.

Q5. Compare RISC and CISC architectures. List at least three differences and explain in which applications each type has an advantage.

Answer: RISC uses simple, fixed-length instructions and relies on compiler optimization, making it faster for pipelining and embedded systems. CISC has complex, variable-length instructions which reduce code size and are better for legacy systems. RISC emphasizes hardware simplicity, while CISC focuses on instruction flexibility.

Q6. What is an interrupt? Explain the sequence of micro-operations in interrupt-driven I/O transfer.

Answer: An interrupt is a signal to the CPU indicating that an I/O device needs attention. When triggered, the CPU completes the current instruction, saves the program counter and status flags, and jumps to the interrupt service routine (ISR). After servicing, it restores the saved context and resumes execution.

Q7. List and explain the categories of registers in the 8086 microprocessor, including the role of segment registers.

Answer: The 8086 has general-purpose registers (AX, BX, CX, DX), segment registers (CS for code, DS for data, SS for stack, ES for extra data), pointer and index registers (SP, BP, SI, DI), and instruction pointer (IP). Segment registers hold base addresses for different memory segments, supporting memory addressing.

Q8. Describe direct and indirect addressing modes with examples from 8086 assembly.

Answer: In direct addressing, the operand address is specified explicitly in the instruction, for example `MOV AX, [1234h]`. In indirect addressing, the instruction uses a register holding the memory address, such as `MOV AX, [BX]`. Indirect addressing is useful for accessing arrays and dynamic data structures.

Q9. Explain the micro-operations needed to fetch an instruction into the Instruction Register (IR). List typical register transfers like MAR ← PC, RD, etc.

Answer: The CPU performs MAR ← PC to place the program counter value into the Memory Address Register. The memory is read (RD) and data is placed in the Memory Data Register (MDR). MDR is then transferred to IR. Finally, PC is incremented to point to the next instruction.

Q10. Write 8086 assembly code to swap two bytes in memory labeled FIRST and SECOND. Explain how the XCHG instruction is used in your solution.

Answer: Example:

```
css
CopyEdit
MOV AL, [FIRST]
XCHG AL, [SECOND]
MOV [FIRST], AL
```

This loads the value at FIRST into AL, exchanges it with SECOND, and stores the swapped value back into FIRST. XCHG simplifies the swap operation without using a temporary memory location.

Chapter 6: Mostly Asked Important Questions – Part C

Q1. Describe the function and structure of the Arithmetic Logic Unit (ALU) in a CPU. Explain how it performs operations such as addition, subtraction, logical AND, and OR.
Answer: The ALU is a core component that executes arithmetic and logical operations. It uses combinational logic circuits such as adders, subtractors, and multiplexers. For addition, it uses a ripple-carry or carry-lookahead adder. Subtraction is performed using two's complement and addition. Logical operations like AND and OR are executed via dedicated logic gates.

Q2. Explain pipelining in a CPU. Describe how instruction execution is divided into stages and analyze its impact on throughput and hazards.
Answer: Pipelining breaks instruction execution into stages like fetch, decode, execute, memory access, and write-back. Each stage processes a different instruction simultaneously, increasing throughput. However, hazards such as data dependencies, control hazards, and structural hazards can occur. Techniques like forwarding, branch prediction, and pipeline stalling are used to manage them.
Q3. What is cache coherence in multiprocessor systems? Explain protocols like MESI and how they ensure consistency across multiple cache copies.
Answer: Cache coherence ensures that multiple processors have consistent views of shared memory. The MESI protocol assigns each cache line a state: Modified, Exclusive, Shared, or Invalid. It uses bus snooping and invalidation messages so that when one core modifies data, other cores either update or invalidate their copies, maintaining coherence.
Q4. Describe the steps involved in translating a virtual address to a physical address using paging. What components are used, and how is the Translation Lookaside Buffer (TLB) involved?
Answer: Virtual address translation involves dividing the virtual address into a page number and an offset. The page number indexes into a page table to retrieve the frame number. The physical address is formed by combining the frame number with the offset. The TLB caches recent translations to expedite this process and reduce memory accesses.
Q5. Explain the difference between write-back and write-through cache policies. Analyze their performance and consistency implications.

Answer: Write-through immediately writes data to both cache and main memory, ensuring consistency but increasing memory traffic. Write-back delays memory updates until the cache block is evicted, reducing memory operations but requiring mechanisms to handle dirty blocks, such as write buffers and cache coherency support.

Q6. Describe the role of control signals in the CPU datapath during instruction execution. Give examples like MemRead, MemWrite, RegDst, ALUSrc, and RegWrite.

Answer: Control signals orchestrate data flow and operation selection in each pipeline stage. MemRead and MemWrite control memory access. RegDst selects the destination register. ALUSrc chooses the second ALU operand between a register and immediate value. RegWrite enables value writing into the register file. These signals are generated by the control unit based on the instruction opcode.

Q7. What is instruction-level parallelism (ILP) and how do superscalar processors exploit it? Illustrate with examples of multiple-issue pipelines.

Answer: ILP refers to executing multiple instructions simultaneously within a single clock cycle. Superscalar processors have multiple functional units and can issue several instructions per cycle. They dynamically schedule independent instructions to different execution units, leveraging techniques like out-of-order execution, register renaming, and branch prediction to maximize throughput.

Q8. Explain the concept of branch prediction in CPUs. Compare static and dynamic prediction methods, and discuss their accuracy consequences.

Answer: Branch prediction aims to guess the outcome of conditional branches to keep the pipeline filled. Static methods use heuristics (e.g., backward branches are taken). Dynamic methods use hardware like 2-bit saturating counters or branch history tables based on runtime behavior. Dynamic prediction adapts to actual patterns, offering higher accuracy and fewer mispredictions.

Q9. Describe Direct Memory Access (DMA). How does it offload work from the CPU, and how does it interact with the memory and bus during data transfer?

Answer: DMA allows peripheral devices to transfer data between memory and I/O without CPU involvement. The CPU sets up the DMA controller with source, destination, and transfer size. The DMA controller then takes control of the system bus, transfers data directly, and interrupts the CPU upon completion. This increases efficiency by reducing CPU load.

Q10. What is microprogramming in CPU control design? Explain how microinstructions are stored and executed to implement the instruction set.

Answer: Microprogramming uses microinstructions stored in a control memory (microcode ROM or writable control store) to generate control signals for each instruction. Each machine instruction maps to a sequence of microinstructions that set the control signals in each clock cycle. This approach simplifies CPU design and allows instruction set updates via microcode changes.

Chapter 7: Mostly Asked Important Questions – Part D

1. Explain how the program counter (PC) and instruction register (IR) work together in the CPU fetch-decode-execute cycle.

Answer: The program counter holds the address of the next instruction to fetch. During the fetch stage, the PC value is transferred to the address bus and memory; the fetched instruction loads into the IR. The PC is then incremented to point to the following instruction. The IR is used during the decode stage to control further processing steps in execution.

2. Describe the structure and working of a barrel shifter. Explain how it can perform multi-bit shifts in one cycle.

Answer: A barrel shifter uses a tree of multiplexers to shift or rotate data bitwise in constant time. By selecting pathways controlled by shift amount bits, it routes inputs to outputs in a single cycle. It enables fast hardware-supported logical and arithmetic shifts without sequential bit shifting.

3. What are system buses in a computer? Explain the differences between data bus, address bus, and control bus, and how bus arbitration is managed.

Answer: The data bus carries actual data between CPU, memory, and I/O. The address bus carries memory addresses from the CPU to memory or peripherals. The control bus carries timing and control signals (e.g., read, write, clock). Bus arbitration prioritizes competing bus requests using daisy-chain or centralized controllers, to prevent conflicts.

4. Explain memory hierarchy in computers. Describe how registers, caches, main memory, and secondary storage differ in speed and size.

Answer: Registers are fastest and smallest, providing immediate CPU access. Cache is next fastest, holding recently used data. Main memory (RAM) is larger but slower. Secondary storage (like HDD/SSD) is much larger and slower. The hierarchy balances speed and capacity to optimize performance and cost.

5. Describe the difference between combinational and sequential circuits. Provide typical examples and explain how each is used in computer design.

Answer: Combinational circuits output values based only on current inputs; examples include adders and multiplexers. Sequential circuits involve memory elements and depend on current input and past state; examples include flip-flops and counters. Combinational logic performs operations, while sequential logic enables stateful control and storage.

6. What is virtual memory? Explain why it is used and describe how page faults are handled in hardware and OS.

Answer: Virtual memory maps program addresses to physical frames using page tables, enabling programs to use more memory than physically available. On a page fault, when a referenced page is not in RAM—the OS pauses execution, loads the page from disk into a free frame (possibly evicting another page), updates the page table, and resumes execution.

7. Explain how an arithmetic adder-subtractor circuit is designed. Describe how it performs both addition and subtraction using two's complement.

Answer: An adder-subtractor uses a full adder with an XOR gate on the second operand controlled by a subtraction line. For subtraction, operand B is inverted, and a '1' is added to implement two's complement as the carry-in. Both operations thus use the same adder structure.

8. Describe the role of the status register or flag register in a CPU. List common flags and provide examples of how they are used in branching decisions.

Answer: The status or flag register holds condition flags: zero (Z), sign (S), carry (C), overflow (V), etc. After arithmetic operations, these flags update. Conditional jump instructions like JZ (jump if zero) or JC (jump if carry) test flags and change program flow accordingly.

9. Explain how the CPU handles multiplication using the shift-and-add method. Describe the steps and the role of accumulator and multiplier registers.

Answer: The shift-and-add multiplier uses a multiplier register and accumulator. For each bit in the multiplier, if the bit is '1', the multiplicand is added to the accumulator. Then both registers are shifted (accumulator–multiplier as a combined register set). This iterates over all bits to compute the product.

10. Describe the role of microinstructions in implementing branch instructions in microprogrammed control. How are conditional and unconditional branches handled?

Answer: In microprogrammed control, each machine instruction corresponds to a sequence of microinstructions. For branches, microinstructions examine condition flags; conditional branches load the microprogram counter (μPC) with a target address only if the condition is met. Unconditional branches use a fixed μPC without condition checking.

Chapter 8: Mostly Asked Important Questions – Part E

1. Explain the concept of clock skew in synchronous systems. How can clock distribution networks and skew management techniques prevent timing failures like hold-time violations.
Answer: Clock skew is the time difference with which a clock signal arrives at sequential elements. Excessive skew can cause hold-time violations or setup-time failures. To mitigate skew, clock distribution networks like balanced H-trees or PLLs are used. Techniques such as intentional skew balancing, insertion buffers, and clock gating ensure timing margins are met across the chip.

2. Describe programmable logic devices such as PALs and CPLDs. How are they configured, and how do they differ from FPGAs in terms of architecture and usage.
Answer: PALs (Programmable Array Logic) and CPLDs (Complex PLDs) are non-volatile devices with fixed OR arrays and programmable AND arrays. They are configured via fuse or anti-fuse programming. FPGAs (Field-Programmable Gate Arrays) have configurable logic blocks and routing fabric, allowing greater flexibility. PALs and CPLDs are ideal for smaller, stable logic tasks, while FPGAs handle complex, reconfigurable systems.

3. What is the role of a branch target buffer (BTB) in modern CPU pipelines? Describe how it stores and predicts branch targets to reduce control hazards.
Answer: A BTB caches the target addresses of recently executed branch instructions. When a branch is fetched, the BTB predicts its target and updates the PC accordingly, reducing pipeline stalls. It stores branch address, target and history bits. This speculation enhances instruction-level parallelism and accuracy of branch prediction.

4. Explain the false sharing problem in multicore cache systems. How does it degrade performance, and what software or hardware techniques are used to resolve it.
Answer: False sharing occurs when multiple cores modify distinct variables in the same cache line, causing unnecessary coherence traffic. Even non-shared data trigger invalidations and cache misses. It degrades performance by increasing latency. Remedies include padding to avoid multiple data in the same cache line and compiler optimizations to align data structures.

5. Describe the difference between fine-grained and coarse-grained multithreading in processor design. What are their respective advantages and trade-offs.
Answer: Fine-grained (interleaved) multithreading switches threads each cycle, hiding pipeline stalls but requiring fast context switching. Coarse-grained switches threads only on long latency events like cache misses, reducing context overhead but less effective at hiding smaller delays. Fine-grained improves throughput, while coarse-grained simplifies hardware.

6. What is vector processing, and how does it differ from scalar processing? Explain how vector registers and pipelines accelerate computations like dot products.
Answer: Vector processors operate on entire arrays of data per instruction using vector registers and pipelines. In contrast, scalar processors handle one data element per instruction. Vector pipelines can perform multiple operations per cycle. For example, dot product is computed via simultaneous multiply-adds across vector lanes, boosting throughput for data-parallel tasks.

7. Explain how error detection and correction codes are implemented in memory systems. Compare parity bits, Hamming codes, and ECC in terms of overhead and correction capability.

Answer: Memory systems use parity bits to detect single-bit errors. Hamming codes can detect and correct single-bit errors and detect double-bit errors with minimal bit overhead. ECC (Error-Correcting Code) like SEC-DED can detect and correct single-bit errors and detect multi-bit errors, with higher overhead. ECC ensures data integrity in critical systems.

8. Describe Tomasulo's algorithm for dynamic instruction scheduling. How does it resolve hazards and enable out-of-order execution using reservation stations and register renaming.
Answer: Tomasulo's algorithm enables out-of-order execution by using reservation stations to buffer operands and instructions. When operands are ready, instructions are issued and executed by functional units. It uses a common data bus to share results. Register renaming eliminates WAR and WAW hazards by mapping architectural registers to physical tags.

9. What is direct memory access (DMA) and how do different DMA modes like burst, cycle stealing, and transparent impact CPU operation and bus availability.

Answer: DMA transfers data without CPU intervention. In burst mode, it monopolizes the bus until transfer completes. Cycle-stealing mode interleaves DMA and CPU, taking control for each cycle. Transparent mode transfers only when CPU is idle. Each mode offers different trade-offs between throughput and CPU performance impact.

10. Explain the concept of superscalar pipeline hazards and how scoreboard techniques manage resource conflicts.

Answer: In superscalar pipelines, multiple instructions are issued per cycle. Hazards include structural (resource contention), data (RAW), and control hazards. Scoreboard techniques dynamically track functional unit usage and operand availability. Instructions are issued only when resources and operands are free, ensuring safe parallel execution.

Chapter 9: Mostly Asked Important Questions – Part F

1. Explain the concept of instruction pipelining in CPUs. Discuss pipeline stages and analyze hazards such as structural, data, and control hazards. How are these hazards resolved.
Answer: Instruction pipelining divides instruction execution into stages such as fetch, decode, execute, memory access, and write-back, allowing multiple instructions to be processed simultaneously. Structural hazards occur when hardware resources are shared, data hazards when instructions depend on previous results, and control hazards during branching. Solutions include forwarding, stalling, branch prediction, and out-of-order execution.

2. Describe associative memory. How is it different from conventional memory, and where is it used in computer systems.
Answer: Associative memory, also called content-addressable memory (CAM), searches for data by content rather than by address. It compares input data with stored data in parallel, enabling fast lookups. CAM is used in cache tag matching, translation lookaside buffers (TLBs), and networking devices for packet filtering.

3. What is memory interleaving. Explain how it improves the performance of memory systems in multiprocessors.
Answer: Memory interleaving splits memory into multiple banks accessed in parallel, allowing simultaneous read/write operations. For example, while one bank is accessed, others can prepare for subsequent operations. It reduces wait cycles and improves bandwidth. In multiprocessors, interleaving reduces contention and increases throughput.

4. Explain the difference between hardwired control and microprogrammed control in CPUs. State advantages and disadvantages of each approach.
Answer: Hardwired control uses fixed logic circuits to generate control signals, offering high speed but inflexibility. Microprogrammed control stores control signals as microinstructions in a control memory, allowing easier modification and complex instruction sets but slower performance. Hardwired is used in RISC processors; microprogrammed is common in CISC designs.

5. Describe the working of a priority encoder. How does it handle multiple active inputs and provide unique output codes.

Answer: A priority encoder assigns priority to inputs and outputs the binary code of the highest-priority active input. It scans inputs from highest to lowest and encodes the first active one it finds. Priority encoders are used in interrupt controllers to resolve multiple simultaneous interrupt requests.

6. What is bus contention in computer systems. Explain how techniques like bus arbitration and bus hierarchies resolve contention.

Answer: Bus contention occurs when multiple devices attempt to use the system bus simultaneously. Bus arbitration assigns control to one device at a time, using techniques like fixed priority, round robin, or daisy chaining. Bus hierarchies organize buses into levels (local, system, backplane) to reduce contention and improve parallelism.

7. Explain the difference between static RAM (SRAM) and dynamic RAM (DRAM). Compare them in terms of structure, speed, cost, and applications.

Answer: SRAM uses flip-flops for each bit, making it faster and requiring no refresh but more expensive and less dense. DRAM stores bits as charges in capacitors, needing periodic refresh but offering higher density and lower cost. SRAM is used for cache; DRAM is used for main memory.

8. What is an instruction set architecture (ISA). Describe how it serves as the interface between hardware and software, and list its key components.

Answer: An ISA defines the set of instructions a CPU can execute, data types, addressing modes, registers, and memory architecture. It allows software developers to write programs independent of underlying hardware implementation. Key components include opcode, operand specifications, and instruction formats.

9. Describe the concept of memory hierarchy in modern computers. How do caches, main memory, and secondary storage work together to optimize performance.

Answer: The memory hierarchy uses fast, small, and expensive memory (registers, caches) close to the CPU, medium-speed main memory (RAM), and large, slow secondary storage (HDD/SSD).

Frequently accessed data is stored in faster memory levels to reduce latency. Caching strategies like LRU and prefetching improve overall system performance.

10. Explain the difference between synchronous and asynchronous data transfers. Provide examples of where each method is used in computer systems.

Answer: In synchronous transfers, data is sent along with a clock signal, ensuring sender and receiver are synchronized (e.g., memory bus transfers). In asynchronous transfers, data uses handshaking signals like request/acknowledge without a global clock (e.g., UART communication). Synchronous is faster but less flexible; asynchronous handles variable speeds and distances better.

Chapter 10: Mostly Asked Important Questions – Part G

1. Explain the role of a control unit in a CPU. How does it coordinate various components during the fetch-decode-execute cycle.

Answer: The control unit manages the flow of data and instructions within the CPU. During the fetch phase, it signals the memory to send the next instruction to the instruction register. In the decode phase, it interprets the opcode and generates control signals to activate the ALU, registers, and memory for execution. This ensures synchronized operation of all CPU components.

2. What is an interrupt vector table. How does the CPU use it to handle multiple interrupt requests.

Answer: The interrupt vector table is a memory-resident table containing the addresses of all interrupt service routines (ISRs). When an interrupt occurs, the CPU uses the interrupt number to index into this table, fetch the ISR address, and transfer control to it. This mechanism supports efficient handling of multiple hardware and software interrupts.

3. Describe the difference between memory-mapped I/O and isolated I/O. Explain the advantages and disadvantages of each approach.

Answer: Memory-mapped I/O uses the same address space for both memory and I/O devices, allowing standard instructions to access devices. Isolated I/O uses a separate address space and special instructions like IN and OUT. Memory-mapped I/O simplifies programming but reduces addressable memory, while isolated I/O preserves memory space but requires dedicated instructions.

4. Explain Booth's algorithm for signed binary multiplication. Provide an example showing how it handles positive and negative operands.

Answer: Booth's algorithm encodes consecutive 1s in the multiplier to reduce the number of additions or subtractions. It scans the multiplier and uses add, subtract, or shift operations based on bit pairs. For example, multiplying +5 and -3 involves encoding -3 and using two's complement arithmetic to compute the product efficiently.

5. What is a stack in computer organization. How are stack operations implemented in hardware using a stack pointer and special instructions.

Answer: A stack is a last-in-first-out (LIFO) memory structure used for temporary storage. It is implemented in hardware using a stack pointer register that tracks the top of the stack. PUSH instructions decrement the stack pointer and store data, while POP increments it and retrieves data. The stack is used for function calls, parameter passing, and storing return addresses.

6. Describe the function of a DMA controller. How does it reduce CPU overhead during data transfers between memory and peripherals.

Answer: The DMA controller manages direct memory access by transferring data between peripherals and memory without CPU intervention. The CPU programs the DMA controller with transfer parameters, then relinquishes bus control. The DMA controller handles the transfer and signals completion via an interrupt, allowing the CPU to perform other tasks concurrently.

7. Explain how parity bits are used for error detection in memory systems. Why can parity not correct errors, and how does ECC improve on this.

Answer: Parity bits indicate whether the number of 1s in a byte is even or odd. On data retrieval, parity is recalculated and compared to the stored parity bit to detect single-bit errors. However, parity cannot locate or correct errors. ECC (Error-Correcting Code) adds redundant bits enabling detection and correction of single-bit errors and detection of multi-bit errors.

8. What are horizontal and vertical microinstructions in microprogramming. Compare their advantages and applications.

Answer: Horizontal microinstructions use wide control words with one bit per control signal, enabling parallel operations but requiring large control memory. Vertical microinstructions use encoded fields and require decoding, reducing memory but increasing execution steps. Horizontal microprogramming is faster; vertical is more compact and suitable for complex instruction sets.

9. Describe how a memory hierarchy uses cache levels (L1, L2, L3) to improve CPU performance. How do write-back and write-through policies affect cache consistency.

Answer: L1 cache is smallest and fastest, L2 larger and slower, and L3 largest but slowest. Together they reduce latency by keeping frequently used data close to the CPU. Write-through updates both cache and main memory immediately, ensuring consistency but with higher traffic. Write-back updates main memory only when cache lines are evicted, reducing traffic but requiring dirty bit management.

10. Explain the concept of instruction pipelining hazards. Provide examples of data, structural, and control hazards and describe methods to resolve them.

Answer: Data hazards occur when instructions depend on the result of previous instructions (e.g., RAW). Structural hazards arise from resource conflicts, and control hazards from branching. Solutions include forwarding (data bypassing), pipeline stalls (bubbles), hardware duplication, and dynamic branch prediction to minimize performance penalties.

Chapter 11: Mostly Asked Important Questions – Part H

1. Explain in detail the steps involved in the instruction fetch-decode-execute cycle of a CPU. How do various components like the program counter, instruction register, ALU, and control unit interact during each stage of this cycle.

Answer: The fetch-decode-execute cycle is the fundamental operation of a CPU that processes instructions. In the fetch stage, the program counter (PC) sends the address of the next instruction to memory, and the fetched instruction is stored in the instruction register (IR). The PC is incremented to point to the following instruction. During decode, the control unit interprets the opcode and generates control signals to route data between registers, the ALU, and memory. In the execute stage, the ALU performs operations like arithmetic or logic, or the CPU interacts with memory or I/O devices as needed. This cycle repeats for each instruction and enables sequential program execution.

2. What is memory hierarchy in modern computer systems. Discuss in detail the different levels such as registers, cache L1, L2, L3, main memory, and secondary storage, including their speeds, sizes, and typical use cases.

Answer: The memory hierarchy organizes storage devices to balance speed, cost, and capacity. Registers are the fastest and smallest, located inside the CPU for immediate data access. L1 cache is small but very fast, followed by L2 and L3 caches that are larger but slower. Main memory RAM provides temporary storage for active programs, while secondary storage HDD or SSD offers persistent, high-capacity storage at much slower speeds. Data frequently moves between levels, with caches storing recently or frequently used data to minimize access times. This layered design optimizes system performance and reduces CPU idle time waiting for data.

3. Describe in detail the working of Booth's algorithm for signed binary multiplication. How does it improve the efficiency of multiplication compared to traditional methods. Provide a step-by-step example with two signed numbers.

Answer: Booth's algorithm reduces the number of additions and subtractions required during multiplication by encoding consecutive 1s in the multiplier. It examines bit pairs in the multiplier to decide whether to add, subtract, or shift. For example, multiplying plus six 0110 by minus three

1101 involves examining bits and applying two's complement arithmetic for subtraction. The result is computed efficiently with fewer operations. This method is particularly advantageous when the multiplier has large blocks of 1s, as it compresses multiple operations into one.

4. Explain in detail how Direct Memory Access DMA works. Discuss its components like the DMA controller, channels, and handshaking signals. How does DMA improve CPU efficiency during I/O operations.

Answer: DMA allows peripherals to transfer data directly to or from memory without CPU involvement. The DMA controller has channels that manage different devices and handshaking signals like request REQ and acknowledge ACK to control bus access. The CPU initializes the DMA controller with the memory address, transfer size, and mode. Once started, the DMA controller takes over the system bus, performs the transfer, and interrupts the CPU when complete. This process reduces CPU overhead, allowing it to focus on computation while data transfers occur in parallel.

5. Compare and contrast RISC Reduced Instruction Set Computer and CISC Complex Instruction Set Computer architectures. Discuss their design philosophies, instruction formats, pipelining efficiency, and typical application domains.

Answer: RISC uses simple, fixed-length instructions optimized for fast execution and efficient pipelining. It requires more instructions to perform complex tasks but achieves higher performance through hardware simplicity and parallelism. CISC uses complex, variable-length instructions, allowing single instructions to perform multi-step operations. RISC is preferred in embedded and mobile systems due to power efficiency, while CISC dominates desktop and server systems for backward compatibility and compact code.

6. Explain in detail the difference between memory-mapped I/O and isolated I/O. How does each method address I/O devices, and what are their advantages and disadvantages in terms of hardware and software complexity.

Answer: Memory-mapped I/O uses the same address space for memory and I/O devices, enabling standard data movement instructions for device access. It simplifies programming but reduces available memory addresses. Isolated I/O uses a separate address space with specialized instructions IN, OUT for I/O operations. It preserves memory space but requires more complex hardware and software to handle separate instruction sets. Memory-mapped I/O is favored in systems with abundant address space, while isolated I/O is common in legacy and constrained systems.

7. What are hazards in instruction pipelining. Discuss the types of hazards structural, data, and control, provide examples of each, and explain how techniques like forwarding, stalling, and branch prediction mitigate these hazards.

Answer: Structural hazards occur when hardware resources are insufficient to handle concurrent instructions, such as two instructions needing the same functional unit. Data hazards happen when one instruction depends on the result of another RAW, WAR, WAW. Control hazards arise from branch instructions disrupting instruction flow. Solutions include forwarding to bypass intermediate stages, inserting pipeline stalls to delay dependent instructions, and using dynamic branch prediction to minimize the impact of control hazards.

8. Describe the role of cache memory in computer systems. Explain the concepts of locality of reference, cache mapping techniques direct, associative, and set-associative, and cache replacement policies like LRU and FIFO.

Answer: Cache memory provides fast access to frequently used data by storing a small portion of main memory. Temporal locality refers to recently accessed data being accessed again soon, and spatial locality refers to accessing data near recently accessed addresses. Direct mapping places each memory block in a fixed cache location, associative mapping allows blocks anywhere, and set-associative mapping combines both approaches. Replacement policies like Least Recently Used LRU and First In First Out FIFO determine which cache block to evict when space is needed.

9. Explain the differences between static RAM SRAM and dynamic RAM DRAM. Discuss their design, speed, power consumption, and usage in different parts of the memory hierarchy.

Answer: SRAM uses flip-flops to store each bit, offering high speed and no refresh requirements but higher cost and lower density. DRAM stores bits as charges in capacitors, requiring periodic refresh but allowing higher densities and lower cost. SRAM is used for caches and registers due to speed, while DRAM is used for main memory due to capacity.

10. Describe in detail how instruction-level parallelism ILP is implemented in modern CPUs. Explain techniques like pipelining, superscalar execution, out-of-order execution, and register renaming.

Answer: ILP executes multiple instructions simultaneously by leveraging hardware features. Pipelining breaks instruction execution into stages. Superscalar CPUs issue multiple instructions per clock cycle. Out-of-order execution allows instructions to execute as soon as operands are ready, rather than waiting for strict program order. Register renaming eliminates false dependencies by assigning different physical registers to logically overlapping variables. Together, these techniques maximize CPU throughput and minimize idle cycles.

Chapter 12: Mostly Asked Important Questions – Part I

1. Explain the concept of virtual memory in detail. How does it allow programs to use more memory than physically available. Discuss the role of page tables, TLBs, and the process of handling a page fault.

Answer: Virtual memory provides an abstraction that allows programs to use a large, continuous address space, even if the physical memory is smaller. The operating system divides virtual memory into pages and maps them to physical frames using page tables. When a program accesses a page not currently in RAM, a page fault occurs. The OS loads the required page from secondary storage into memory, updates the page table, and resumes execution. A Translation Lookaside Buffer (TLB) caches recent page table entries for faster lookups, reducing the overhead of address translation.

2. Describe in detail the process of instruction pipelining in CPUs. Explain each stage of a five-stage pipeline and how it improves instruction throughput. Also discuss how pipeline hazards are detected and resolved.

Answer: Instruction pipelining divides instruction execution into stages such as fetch, decode, execute, memory access, and write-back. Each stage processes a different instruction simultaneously, increasing throughput. Hazards disrupt the smooth flow of instructions. Structural hazards arise from hardware resource conflicts, data hazards from operand dependencies, and control hazards from branching. Techniques like hardware duplication, forwarding, stalling, and branch prediction mitigate these hazards and maintain pipeline efficiency.

3. What is cache memory. Discuss the principles of temporal and spatial locality and how they influence cache performance. Explain cache mapping techniques and cache replacement policies with examples.

Answer: Cache memory is a small, high-speed storage between the CPU and main memory, holding frequently accessed data. Temporal locality means recently used data is likely to be reused soon, and spatial locality refers to accessing data near recently accessed addresses. Direct mapping assigns each block to a fixed cache location, associative mapping allows blocks anywhere, and set-associative mapping provides a compromise. Replacement policies like Least Recently Used (LRU) evict the least used block, while First-In-First-Out (FIFO) removes the oldest.

4. Explain how a microprogrammed control unit works. Compare it with a hardwired control unit and discuss their relative advantages and disadvantages.
Answer: A microprogrammed control unit stores control signals as microinstructions in a control memory. Each machine instruction corresponds to a sequence of microinstructions that generate the necessary control signals for execution. Hardwired control units use combinational logic to generate control signals directly. Microprogrammed units are easier to design and modify but slower due to memory access delays. Hardwired units are faster but inflexible, requiring redesign for instruction set changes.

5. Describe in detail how a CPU handles interrupts. Explain the steps involved from the moment an interrupt is raised to the execution of the corresponding Interrupt Service Routine (ISR).
Answer: When an interrupt is raised, the CPU finishes the current instruction, disables further interrupts, and saves the program counter and processor state. It fetches the ISR address from the interrupt vector table and transfers control to the ISR. After servicing, the CPU restores the saved state and re-enables interrupts. This process allows the CPU to handle asynchronous events while preserving program execution.

6. What is memory interleaving. Explain its types and how it improves memory access speed in multiprocessor systems. Provide an example of a two-way interleaved memory system.
Answer: Memory interleaving divides memory into multiple banks accessed in parallel. In high-order interleaving, consecutive memory blocks are placed in the same bank, while in low-order interleaving, blocks are distributed across banks. This allows simultaneous access to different banks, improving bandwidth. For example, in two-way interleaving, odd and even addresses go to separate banks, enabling parallel access to consecutive addresses.

7. Compare synchronous and asynchronous data transfer methods. Discuss their working mechanisms, advantages, disadvantages, and examples of where each is used.

Answer: Synchronous transfers use a shared clock signal to coordinate data exchange, ensuring precise timing. It is faster and used in memory systems but less flexible for devices with variable speeds. Asynchronous transfers rely on handshaking signals like request and acknowledge, allowing devices to operate independently of a clock. It is used in serial communication such as UART. Synchronous systems are suitable for high-speed, short-distance transfers; asynchronous systems handle long-distance and variable-speed devices better.

8. Describe the difference between Harvard and Von Neumann architectures. Explain how Harvard architecture improves performance and mention practical systems where it is used.

Answer: Von Neumann architecture uses a single memory for instructions and data, creating a bottleneck as only one can be accessed at a time. Harvard architecture separates instruction and data memory with independent buses, allowing simultaneous fetch and data operations, improving throughput. Harvard architecture is used in digital signal processors (DSPs) and embedded systems requiring high-speed real-time performance.

9. Explain in detail the operation of a DMA controller. Discuss different DMA transfer modes such as burst mode, cycle stealing, and transparent mode, and analyze their impact on system performance.

Answer: A DMA controller manages data transfers between peripherals and memory without CPU intervention. In burst mode, it transfers a block of data in one go, blocking the CPU from bus access. Cycle stealing allows the DMA controller to transfer data one word at a time, temporarily pausing CPU bus access. Transparent mode transfers data only when the CPU is idle. Burst mode maximizes transfer speed but can stall the CPU, while cycle stealing and transparent mode balance CPU and I/O performance.

10. What is Tomasulo's algorithm. Explain how it allows out-of-order execution in CPUs and resolves data hazards using reservation stations and register renaming.

Answer: Tomasulo's algorithm schedules instructions dynamically using reservation stations to hold operands until they are ready. Register renaming prevents false dependencies (WAR and WAW hazards) by assigning new physical registers for each write. When operands become available on the common data bus (CDB), waiting instructions execute out-of-order without violating program correctness. This approach maximizes instruction throughput and efficiently uses CPU resources.

Chapter 13: Mostly Asked Important Questions – Part J

1. Explain the concept of instruction-level parallelism in modern processors. Discuss the techniques used to exploit ILP such as pipelining, superscalar architecture, out-of-order execution, and dynamic scheduling. How do these techniques improve CPU throughput.
Answer: Instruction-level parallelism ILP allows multiple instructions to be executed simultaneously, improving CPU throughput. Pipelining breaks instruction execution into stages so multiple instructions overlap in different stages. Superscalar processors issue multiple instructions per clock cycle using multiple execution units. Out-of-order execution allows instructions to execute as soon as operands are ready rather than in strict program order. Dynamic scheduling and techniques like Tomasulo's algorithm resolve data hazards and manage resources efficiently. Together, these techniques maximize utilization of CPU components and reduce idle cycles.

2. Describe in detail the working of a control bus, data bus, and address bus in a computer system. How do these buses interact during memory read and write operations.
Answer: The address bus carries the memory address from CPU to memory or I/O devices, specifying the location for read or write. The data bus transfers data between CPU, memory, and peripherals. The control bus carries control signals like read, write, clock, and interrupt requests. During a memory read, the CPU places the address on the address bus, activates the read signal on the control bus, and retrieves data over the data bus. In a memory write, data is placed on the data bus, and the write signal is activated to store data in the specified location.

3. Explain in detail how paging works in virtual memory systems. Discuss the role of page tables, page frames, TLBs, and how page faults are handled by the operating system.
Answer: Paging divides virtual memory into fixed-size pages and physical memory into page frames. The page table maps virtual pages to physical frames. When the CPU generates a virtual address, the page number is translated into a frame number, and the offset is added to get the physical address. The Translation Lookaside Buffer TLB caches recent page table entries for faster lookups. If the page is not in memory, a page fault occurs, and the OS loads the page from disk into a free frame, updates the page table, and resumes execution.

4. Compare static and dynamic RAM in detail. Explain their design, advantages, disadvantages, and typical applications in a computer system.
Answer: Static RAM SRAM uses flip-flops to store data, offering high speed and no refresh requirement. It is more expensive and consumes more power, making it suitable for small, fast memory like CPU caches. Dynamic RAM DRAM stores data as charges in capacitors, requiring periodic refresh, but it is cheaper and denser, making it ideal for main memory. SRAM provides faster access but is less scalable, while DRAM balances cost and capacity for large memory systems.

5. What is an interrupt in computer systems. Explain in detail the difference between vectored and non-vectored interrupts and how priority is managed in a system with multiple devices.
Answer: An interrupt signals the CPU to pause its current task and execute an Interrupt Service Routine ISR. In vectored interrupts, the address of the ISR is provided by the interrupting device or stored in an interrupt vector table. In non-vectored interrupts, the CPU jumps to a predefined ISR address. When multiple devices raise interrupts simultaneously, priority is managed using hardware or software schemes such as daisy chaining, priority encoders, or interrupt priority levels to ensure critical devices are serviced first.

6. Explain in detail the difference between synchronous and asynchronous serial data communication. Provide examples of devices that use each method and discuss their advantages and limitations.
Answer: In synchronous communication, data is transmitted along with a shared clock signal, ensuring precise timing. It is faster and used in systems like memory buses. Asynchronous communication uses start and stop bits with no shared clock, allowing devices to operate at independent speeds. UART serial ports use asynchronous communication. Synchronous communication is efficient for high-speed short-distance transfers, while asynchronous systems are better suited for variable-speed, long-distance communication.

7. Describe in detail the difference between RISC and CISC architectures. Explain how instruction set complexity, addressing modes, and execution speed differ between the two and their implications for compiler design.

Answer: RISC architectures use simple, fixed-length instructions with few addressing modes, enabling faster execution and efficient pipelining. Compilers for RISC must generate more instructions to accomplish complex tasks. CISC architectures use complex, variable-length instructions with many addressing modes, allowing single instructions to perform multi-step operations. CISC compilers generate fewer instructions but require more hardware complexity for decoding. RISC is preferred in modern mobile and embedded systems for power efficiency, while CISC dominates desktop and server environments for compatibility and compact code size.

8. Explain in detail how a CPU performs multiplication using the shift-and-add method. Provide a step-by-step example to illustrate the process.

Answer: In the shift-and-add method, the CPU examines each bit of the multiplier. For each bit set to 1, the multiplicand is shifted left by the bit's position and added to the result. For bits set to 0, no addition is performed. For example, multiplying 5 (101) by 3 (011), the CPU adds shifted values of the multiplicand where multiplier bits are 1. This method simplifies multiplication using repeated addition and shifting.

9. Discuss the concept of bus contention in detail. Explain how arbitration methods like daisy chaining, centralized arbitration, and distributed arbitration resolve contention in multi-device systems.

Answer: Bus contention occurs when multiple devices attempt to use the system bus simultaneously. Daisy chaining assigns priority based on physical connection order; higher priority devices nearer the controller get bus access first. Centralized arbitration uses a single arbiter to grant access based on predefined policies like fixed priority or round-robin. Distributed arbitration lets devices negotiate bus access among themselves. These methods ensure orderly access and prevent conflicts.

10. Explain how multi-level caches L1, L2, and L3 work together in modern processors. Discuss their size, speed, and how they help minimize memory access latency.

Answer: L1 cache is the smallest and fastest, located closest to the CPU cores for immediate data access. L2 cache is larger but slower, serving as a backup for L1 misses. L3 cache is shared among cores, larger, and slower than L2, but still much faster than main memory. Together, these caches exploit locality of reference, reduce memory latency, and ensure the CPU spends less time waiting for data from slower memory.

9 789369 917921

Printed at Repro India Ltd.